A GEMSTONE ADVENTURE

Prince Gem of Ology's Royal Quest

written & illustrated by
Yvonne Jones

For my better half. Thank you for always believing in me. – Y.J.

No part of this publication may be reproduced in whole or in part, or stored in a retrieval system, or transmitted in any form or by any means, electronic, mechanical, photocopying, recording, or otherwise, without written permission of the publisher. For information regarding permission, write to LHC Publishing.

ISBN-10: 0997025433
ISBN-13: 978-0-9970254-3-9

Text & Illustration copyright © 2016 by Yvonne Jones

All rights reserved. Published by LHC Publishing

Printed in the U.S.A.

Beyond the woods, beyond the seas, beyond high mountains a long, long time ago, there was a beautiful and prosperous little kingdom named **Paragon**. As it was custom for all Kings-to-be in the land of **Paragon**, Prince **Gem of the House of Ology** had to set out to begin his grand quest. Success in this quest would bring great honor upon him.

"Prince **Gem of Ology**," the royal magister said. "Here is what you shall seek. You will do well if you remember all that you have learned during your studies."

Though he wasn't good at potions in alchemy, the Prince had been exceptional at runes and the many uses for gems and jewels. He would much rather have been an excellent swordsman, but he couldn't help it. He loved gemstones.

Lifting his arm, the old man handed the Prince a rolled up parchment.

Prince **Gem of Ology** unrolled it carefully, took a deep breath and read:

Glory you seek,
And glory you shall find.
If out you set
And ten gemstones you mind.

Ten in number,
No more, no less.
This rhyme shall list them,
So you need not guess.

Diamond and Ruby,
Amethyst and Pearl.
Emerald and Turquoise,
The dream of every girl.

Sapphire and Opal
Are gemstones eight and nine.
Topaz and Jade,
And the triumph shall soon be thine.

Prince **Gem of Ology** was familiar with all but a few of these listed gemstones, rare mineral crystals valued for their beauty. His stomach buzzed with nerves and he frowned.

"Magister **Krustallos**," he called. "**Diamonds**, **Rubies**, **Sapphires** and **Emeralds** I recognize as precious jewels from my lessons. Though not a crystal, even the precious value of a **Pearl** is beknoweth to me. But what are these other names mentioned here?"

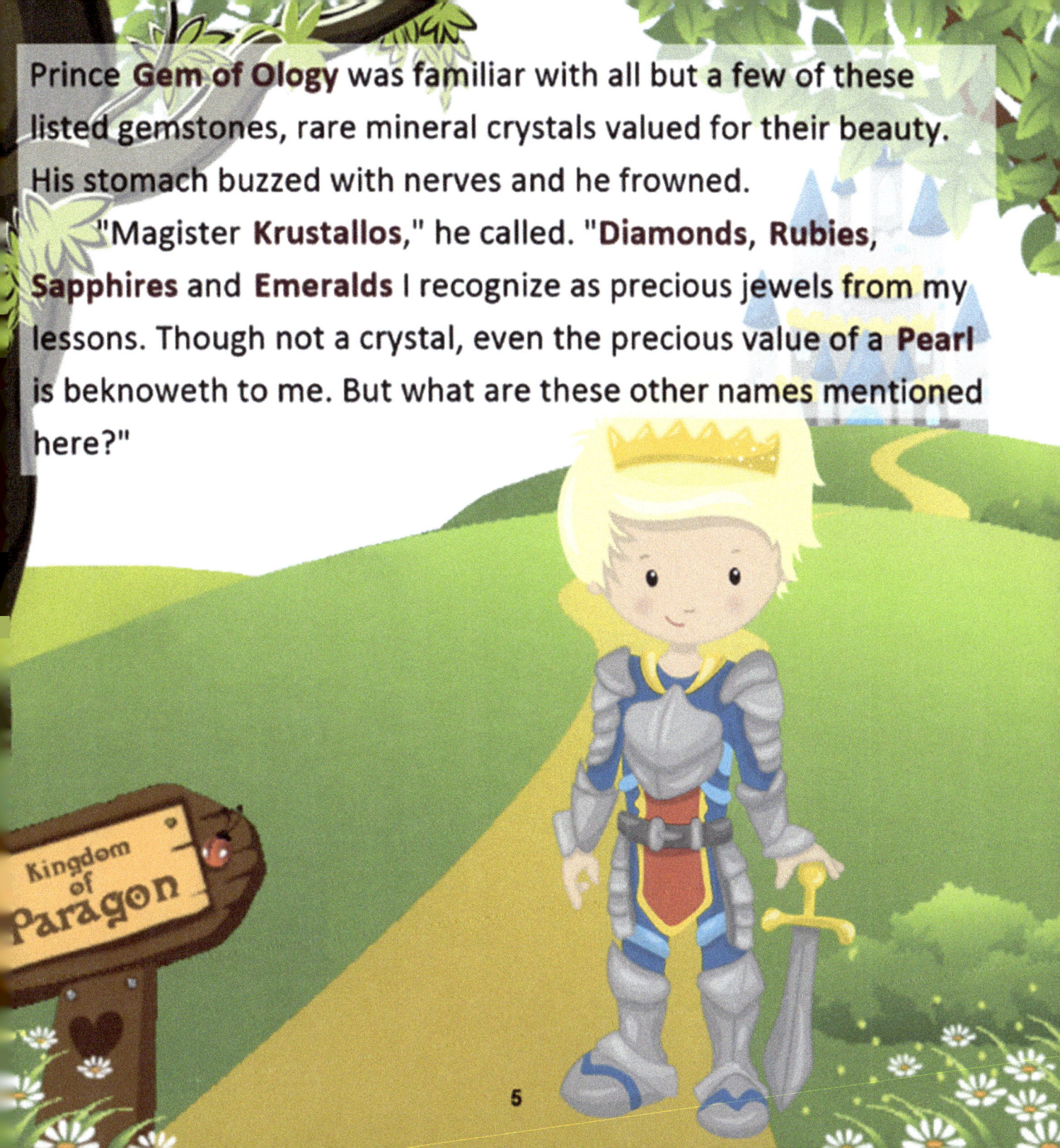

"These, my dear Prince, are semiprecious stones. Albeit this lexis, they are most valued by many and should therefore not be missed. Now go! Make haste so you will return by sundown in time for your most important of days." The old man handed the prince a little scroll that was meant to help him with the first part of his royal quest.

Prince **Gem of Ology** fetched his horse from the royal stables, mounted it, and was off to venture outside the kingdom's gates. He unfurled the little scroll and read:

> Formed in the Earth's mantle deep beneath
> Under great pressure and incredible heat.
> Through volcanic eruption to the surface it came,
> 'Unbreakable' is the Greek meaning of its name.
> It's the hardest of all substances known,
> For made out of carbon is this precious stone.

Prince **Gem of Ology** immediately knew that this verse was about a **Diamond**. And he knew exactly where to find one.

He rode his horse over rolling meadows, across raging waters, and through high-ranging mountains until he reached the realm of **Adamas**, a region known for the most precious and brilliant **Diamonds** in all of **Paragon**.

A noble, elderly steward was already awaiting his arrival. "Welcome, Your Highness," he said with a deep respectful bow. "And my compliments to you. **Adamas** is the ancient Greeks' word for 'unbreakable,' which describes a diamond perfectly. By coming here, you have solved the first part of your quest.

The Prince felt quite proud of himself. *I can do this*, he thought. Maybe he'll even be the fastest ever to complete this royal and traditional quest.

The steward handed Prince **Gem of Ology** a little velvet pouch. In it was the most precious and sparkly **Diamond** the Prince had ever seen. After the Prince placed the pouch safely under his saddle, the steward handed him a scroll that would help him find the next gem of his pursuit.

Still on his horse, **Prince Gem of Ology** made haste to find out more about the ensuing quest. Unfolding his new scroll, he read:

> Hosted in marble within the Earth,
> To this day lays mystery around the origin of its birth.
> A type of Corundum - a rare mineral, indeed,
> Laced with Chromium to give it its dazzling bleed.
> ´Red´ is the Latin meaning of its name,
> The ´King of Precious Stones´ for some cultures it became.

Corundum? the Prince thought. That could be a **Ruby** or a **Sapphire**, for both are made of this very rare mineral. But he remembered something else: **Rubies** and **Sapphires** are identical, except in their color. Only **Rubies** are red. All other colors are **Sapphires**. There was no doubt in his mind to where he had to go.

"Off to the vale of **Mogok**!" Prince **Gem of Ology** commanded his horse. **Mogok** was known as the Legendary Valley of **Rubies** in the kingdom of **Paragon**. It was the source of many of the world's most famous gems.

Along steep and lush ridges Prince **Gem of Ology** rode his noble stallion beneath the day's burning sun. No time was to be wasted if he wanted to return to the castle before nightfall.

The Prince turned a bend. Although impossible, as he had the swiftest and most skilled horse in the land, he came upon the same steward he had left behind in **Adamas**. How could this be?

"Most welcome, my Prince," the steward greeted him once more. "This task too you have mastered by coming to this very place." With a bow, he handed Prince **Gem of Ology** a pillow upon which sat a deep-red gem - the most beautiful **Ruby** he had ever laid his eyes on; its rich color evoking the most intense emotions beknoweth to mankind.

Bedazzled by its splendor, he placed the precious stone into the velvet pouch that already held the **Diamond**. Then, the Prince accepted the small scroll the steward offered him and got back on his way to solve the next part of his quest.

Prince **Gem of Ology** unrolled his third piece of paper. Eagerly, he read:

> A hexagonal prism, with six equal sides,
> As the most valued form of the Beryl mineral it strides.
> 'Green Gem' is the Greek meaning of its name,
> Chromium's trace helped it advance to this fame.
> Its deep and rich color makes it valuable and rare,
> This precious gemstone Kings and Queens would wear.

The Prince smiled. These were very good hints, indeed. The most valued form of the **Beryl** mineral was the **Emerald**. The Prince loved its rich green, for this was one of his favorite colors. So off he went on his trusted horse, making his way to a village named **Smaragdus**. He was sure that this was the right site to go to, for **Smaragdus** meant 'Green Precious Stone' in the ancient Greek language.

The royal magister had been right! He really *did* need his studies for this quest. Luckily, the Prince was good at ancient Greek. But he sure hoped he wouldn't have to remember anything from his *Paragonian Architecture Through the Ages*, as this was his worst subject.

Over grassy meadows and green pastures he rode, confident that he would soon be holding his latest treasure in his hands.

Soon thereafter, he pulled the reins of his horse, bringing them to a stop before an enormous hedge of wild undergrowth. Before him was a wall of lush and green bushes, no doubt meant to protect **Smaragdus**, home of the most beautiful **Emeralds** within the kingdom of **Paragon**. Dismounting his horse, the Prince drew his sword and began to hack his way through the thicket. Tired and sweaty, he became quite anxious, as this was wasting valuable time.

Finally, Prince **Gem of Ology** made his way to the other side of the enormous hedge, where once more, the faithful steward was awaiting him.

"Bravo!" the steward exclaimed after seeing the Prince push through the hedge. How did he get here so fast? "You solved this third part of your quest and shall now receive your reward." He handed him a red cushion upon which sat a breathtaking **Emerald**. It sparkled and beautifully reflected the sun's glistening rays.

With delight, Prince **Gem of Ology** plucked the gem from its place and carefully placed it into his little velvet pouch. Now he had a **Diamond**, a **Ruby** and an **Emerald**. All three were very precious stones.

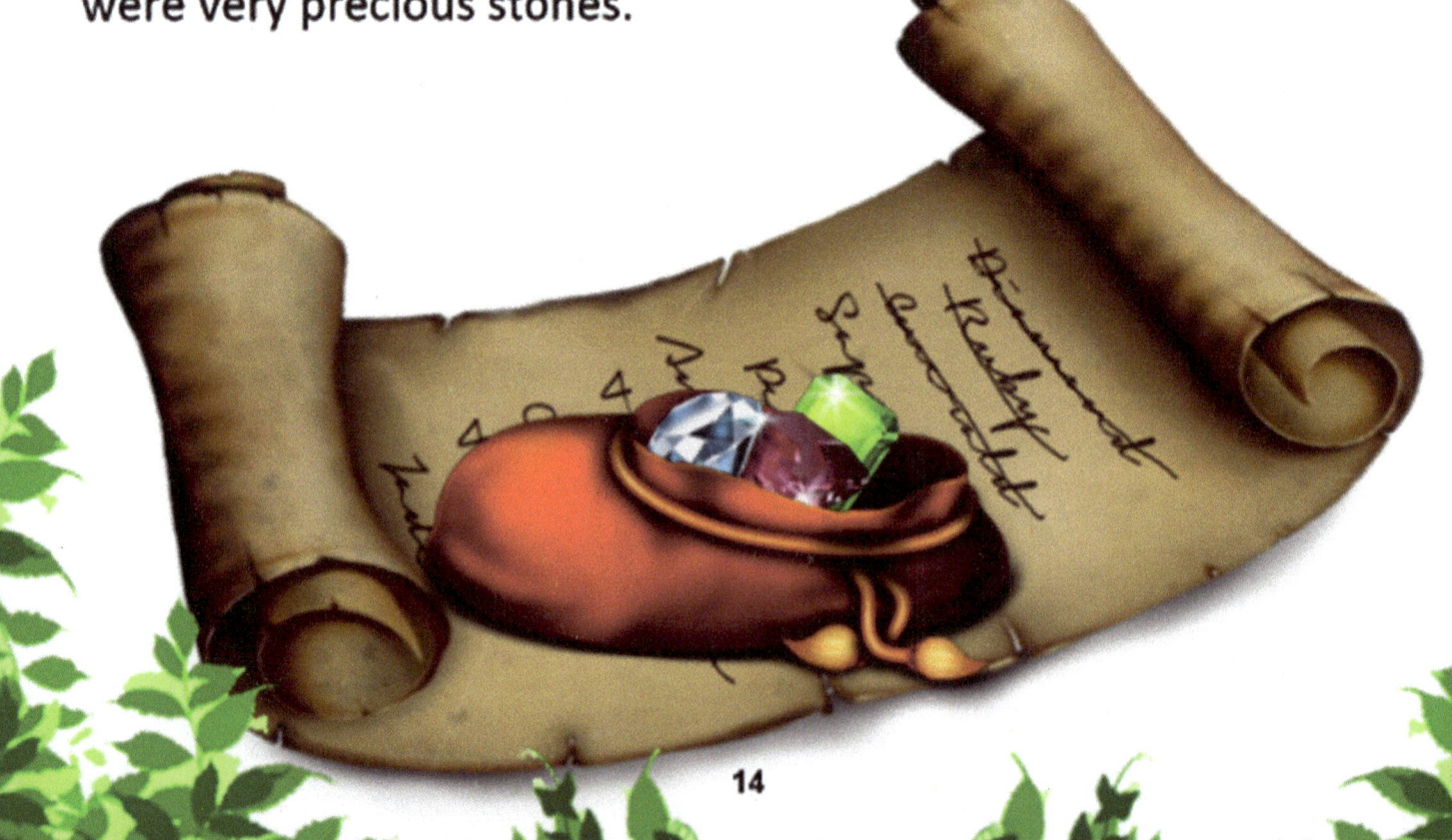

After Prince **Gem of Ology** accepted the next little scroll from the steward to find his fourth gemstone, he climbed onto his horse.

Sitting astride his steed, he carefully opened the piece of paper and read:

> Shades of purple, lilac and mauve,
> This semiprecious stone can be found in many a trove.
> The most valued Quartz variety it represents,
> The effect of poison folklore says it amends.
> Its wine-like color gave the gem its name,
> As 'Protection from Drunkenness' to the Greeks it became.

"Oh, I remember this lesson well," Prince **Gem of Ology** said to the steward. "See you in **Bacchus**, home of the most prized **Amethysts** within all of **Paragon**!"

With that, the Prince and his horse galloped east toward **Bacchus**, beknoweth to all as the name for the Roman god of wine.

Reaching the realm of **Bacchus**, Prince **Gem of Ology** found three beautiful wooden chests sitting on top of a table. Each had a different pattern skillfully carved into its lid.

The first displayed an octahedron - a shape with two pyramids, their four-sided bottoms touching.

The second chest had a hexagonal prism on the top, a structure with six identical sides.

The third box also showed a six-sided prism, but six-sided pyramids were etched onto both ends of it.

Prince **Gem of Ology** flinched as a voice said, "Choose your chest wisely, for you can do so only once." It was the steward who, again, already awaited the Prince.

Prince **Gem of Ology** smiled. He knew that the first shape, an octahedron, was the typical form of a **Diamond**. The second shape, a hexagonal prism, was an attribute of **Beryl**, the mineral a precious **Emerald** is made of. This left him with the third chest, which held the prismatic bipyramidal shape. The Prince gently picked up the last chest and opened it very slowly. In it, he found a beautiful and breathtaking **Amethyst**. Its purple hue playfully reflected the sun's light.

Prince **Gem of Ology** carefully lifted the jewel out of its chest and placed it into his velvet pouch beneath his horse's saddle that held all other stones he had found so far.

"You truly know the structure of these prized crystals, my Prince!" the steward commended. "So on you shall ride to fulfill your destiny." With these words, he handed the Prince the next scroll.

PPrince **Gem of Ology** once again mounted his horse, unrolled the scroll and read:

> Not quite a crystal, but precious still,
> It became the most beloved gem at Kings' and Queens' will.
> Formed within mollusks' very soft tissue,
> The organic gem occurs in many a hue.
> Most valuable when in a perfect, round shape,
> It is composed of calcium carbonate.

   Now this one the Prince didn't have to think about; all other gemstones described in his poem were inorganic except one: the precious **Pearl**. Whilst still considered a gemstone, **Pearls** are organic, made by a living organism.
   Looking at his map, his eyes fell on the borough of **Momme**. And this was exactly where he had to go, for he knew **Momme** was the term used to describe the standard unit for measuring

a **Pearl**'s weight.

After many a mile on the back of his horse, Prince **Gem of Ology** finally entered the realm of **Momme**. Hearing the waves of the ocean, he could smell the briny sea air. Seagulls were squawking up above him. Again, the elderly steward was already awaiting his arrival.

"I see you have found your way to our precious **Momme**, dear Prince. As the region with the kingdom's most scenic ponds, lakes and seas, it embodies the mystery and power of water, which gave rise to all of our highly treasured **Pearls**."

Handing him a perfectly round and shiny **Pearl**, the steward continued, "You have done very well on your quest so far, Your Highness. Not long now until you shall return home victorious."

Grateful and with utmost care, Prince **Gem of Ology** accepted the flawless **Pearl** and added it to his collection.

Sitting back on his brawny stallion, the Prince unfurled the scroll he had just received from the steward and read:

> Forming only in earth's most dry and barren of regions,
> The shade is what defines the name of these unforgettable gems.
> 'Turkish Stone' is the meaning of its name,
> Embedded in its host-rock this sky-blue stone became.
> Acid groundwater is what seeps into the earth,
> Reacting with minerals to give rise to this gem's birth.

These clues Prince **Gem of Ology** recognized immediately, for they described his most favored gemstone of all: the sky-blue **Turquoise**. It wasn't as shiny or sparkly as other gemstones, but it was an unforgettable and rich color.

The Prince knew that the region he had to travel to this time was called **Mefkat**, for this was the name ancient Egyptians used for **Turquoise**.

Riding his horse from the seaside many miles through dry and barren lands, **Prince Gem of Ology** finally reached an enormous boulder within the land of **Mefkat**. There were three small openings in the rock's surface, big enough to reach inside. Above each opening hung a small wooden sign.

The first sign read '**Aqua Blue**,' the second '**Persian Blue**' and the third '**Robin Blue**.'

"Greetings, my noble Majesty," a familiar voice exclaimed. Stepping out from behind the boulder was the elderly steward yet again.

'How could the steward possibly have passed me?' Prince **Gem of Ology** thought. He was sure he took the main road; the fastest and most direct route.

"Before you are three wooden signs," the steward continued. "Only one holds the true name used for a beautiful and richly colored **Turquoise**. Choose wisely, for you get to do so only once."

Prince **Gem of Ology** beamed with confidence, as he knew without a doubt which name to choose. His mother, the Queen, had a beautiful pair of pendant earrings with these magnificent stones that she only wore to special occasions and ceremonies. Having admired them many times before, he knew that a truly blue **Turquoise** was called '**Persian Blue**.'

Stepping toward the second opening, Prince **Gem of Ology** lowered his hand slowly into it. His fingers made out a strange shape within the rock. Clasping the object, he pulled it out of the hollow. In his hands, he found something unexpected: an old-fashioned skeleton key.

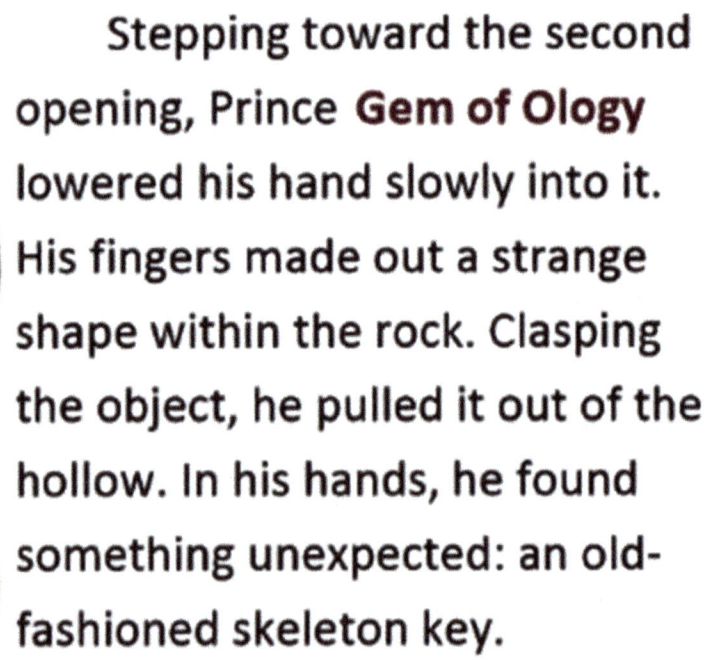

Presenting a tray with a breathtaking **Turquoise** upon it, the steward said, "Once again, you have applied well what you have learned, my Prince. Take this stone as your reward. As for the key, safekeep it for you will need it in a short while."

With that, the steward gave Prince **Gem of Ology** his next parchment and next clue.

The Prince read:

> Every color but red this precious gemstone can be,
> For if it were red, it would be titled a Ruby.
> Most precious and valuable in the color of blue,
> For 'Blue Stone' is what its ancient Greek name means, too.
> Just like a Ruby it is a type of Corundum,
> Turning deep blue when combined with Iron and Titanium.

Because of his peculiar interests, Prince **Gem of Ology** had a wealth of knowledge about precious gemstones. He knew that both **Rubies** and **Sapphires** were a type of the **Corundum** mineral. As he had already found a beautiful **Ruby** within the valley of **Mogok**, this rhyme had to describe a **Sapphire**.

So off he went, dashing toward the dale of **Ceylon**, a region known within the Kingdom of **Paragon** for its abundance of beautiful **Sapphires**.

Crossing rushing brooks and whispering streams, Prince **Gem of Ology** at last made it to a wide and lovely clearing. Before him loomed an enormous wall, encircling the entire valley of **Ceylon**. To enter it, the Prince had to pass through one

of two heavy, wooden gates. Each gate held a sign; one blue, one red.

"You have come quite far, my Prince," a familiar voice spoke behind him. Yet again, the steward had made it to the site before Prince **Gem of Ology**. He continued, "Using the wisdom of the rhyme, open the proper gate with the key you previously received. Choose right, and you will obtain your desired gem."

Taking a moment to ponder his choices, Prince **Gem of Ology** said with conviction, "A **Sapphire** can be any color but red, for if it were red, it would be a **Ruby**." With that, he took the skeleton key he obtained in the land of **Mefkat**, placed it into the blue door's key hole and slowly turned it. To his great relief, the lock came undone and the door creaked open. Behind it, Prince **Gem of Ology** found a cushion with the brightest and bluest **Sapphire** he'd ever laid his eyes on. He plucked the precious stone from the cushion and placed it in his little bag.

Returning to his horse, he looked around, but could not make out the steward's whereabouts. Resting atop his saddle, however, lay a small scroll, listing anew a number of hints to find the next gem.

Prince **Gem of Ology** took the scroll and unrolled it. He was getting a bit nervous, as he was now going to have to identify semiprecious stones, gems he didn't know much about.

> With its splendid play of colors, it's the most unusual of gems,
> For its hue this stone is able to evermore change.
> A creation of seasonal rains that drenched dry ground,
> Once the water evaporated, deposits of silica could be found.
> Forming the gem so colorful and bright,
> Able like no other in diffracting light.

Prince **Gem of Ology** fathomed that this verse was describing an **Opal**, for only an **Opal** displayed an ever changing set of colors. Looking at his map, however, he frowned at the page. He was quite uncertain where to go next to find this vibrant and beloved gem. One of the regions on the map was named **Kupa-Piti**. During his studies the Prince had learned that **Coober Pedy** was considered to be the **Opal** capital of the world. Could it be that **Kupa-Piti** and **Coober Pedy** described the same place? He wouldn't be sure unless he continued on his way, so on his horse he climbed to resume his quest.

Over steep hills and vast valleys Prince **Gem of Ology** rode until he came upon a clearing. In the middle stood his trusted steward.

"Dear Prince," the steward greeted him with a big smile. "I see you have made it to **Coober Pedy**, also called **Kupa-Piti**, which means "Boy's Waterhole" in this region's local language. Now it is up to you to find your treasured **Opal**.

Looking around the clearing, Prince **Gem of Ology** spotted a hoary well. Without hesitation, he scampered toward it and peered down its deep opening. Complete darkness filled the well's shaft. A wooden bucket was attached to the end of a long and heavy rope. Prince **Gem of Ology** grabbed the rope and strenuously pulled on it, the bucket clanking against the well's wall as it made its way up. As it reached the rim of the well, a breathtaking **Opal** revealed itself in the vessel, sparkling with every imaginable color within the sun's light. The Prince took hold of the gem and dropped it carefully into his small pouch.

Beaming with joy, he turned to face the steward once again, who was already preparing to present the next scroll.

The shadows of the trees began to deepen. The day was slowly coming to an end. The Prince's time was running out. Atop his horse, Prince **Gem of Ology** opened up the small piece of paper and read:

> Though most commonly found in golden yellow,
> This radiant gem appears in all shades of the rainbow.
> Highly priced for its exceptional brilliance and shine.
> Its name means "Yellow Burn" and was thought quite divine.
> Formed during magma cooling within igneous stone,
> This gem was chipped away to expose a translucent tone.

"Yellow?" the Prince pondered, trying to remember what he had learned. The "Yellow Burn" gave away that this verse was about a **Topaz**. And in order to find himself the most valuable and rarest **Topaz** within all of **Paragon**, he had to make his way to the realms of **Capao**, a region known for this yellow gem.

No time was to be wasted, as most of the day's light had already been burnt. Riding his horse through thick and lush forests all the way to **Capao**, Prince **Gem of Ology**'s path was crossed by another, leaving him with three possible ways upon which to continue his travels. A wooden signpost stood beside the crosswalk, with each sign pointing in a different direction.

"**Sherry Topaz**?" he pondered aloud, reading the first sign. He knew that this **Topaz** variety was light orange-brown in color, so not the one he was looking for. The second sign read '**Mystic Topaz**.' This type, the Prince knew, was multicolored, with a rainbow-like effect. That left him with the third and final sign on the wooden post. On it, the words '**Imperial Topaz**' were written. Eagerly, he guided his horse down the path following the last sign's direction, for he knew that the golden-yellow **Imperial Topaz** was the rarest and most valuable of all. Considered to be the color of the setting sun, it received its name from a Russian Tsar, who claimed exclusive rights to this gemstone.

Prince **Gem of Ology** didn't have to ride for very long until he came upon a large wooden trunk in the middle of his path. Upon lifting its lid, he made out the most striking **Topaz** he had ever seen, glistening in the evening's setting sun. The Prince gently plucked the gem from its place, put it in his pouch and took hold of the scroll that also lay in the box. He looked around, but strangely, there was no sign of the elderly steward anywhere.

One more, he thought blissfully, climbing back onto his horse.

Unrolling a scroll for this journey's very last time, Prince **Gem of Ology** read:

> A symbol of "Heaven" this gem represents,
> As a circular disc in oriental hands.
> The healer of kidneys it was known by all,
> So "Stone of the Hip" this gem they would call.
> In a variety of colors, green most valued and mused,
> For ancient carvings this stone was commonly used.

This is my final gem to find, the Prince thought. And the only gem left on his list was the beautiful **Jade**. He had to hurry, so that he may return home before the day's end. The sun was about to set and rest for the day to come. If it did before he returned, he would fail. The Prince felt quite discouraged.

Looking at his map, Prince **Gem of Ology** spotted the land of **Maori**, a people within the Kingdom of **Paragon** that esteemed **Jade** to its highest. Gently nudging his tiring horse, the Prince resumed his voyage, riding across beautiful meadows amidst sweet smelling and vibrant flowers into the region of **Maori**. In the middle of the field, the Prince came upon an old tree stump. On top of the stump lay seven wooden blocks, each engraved with a letter.

"One final quest, my dear Prince!" Prince **Gem of Ology** heard a voice say behind him. Turning around, he saw the stout little steward once again. With an encouraging smile, the old man continued, "Before you are letters A, N, P, U, O, M and U. Arrange them in such a way, that they will spell the word used for **Jade** throughout the **Maori** region. If you succeed, I shall send you on your way home faster than your horse could ever carry you."

The sun slowly began to disappear behind the vast horizon. Prince **Gem of Ology**'s time was about to run out.

Thinking urgently about his task, the Prince looked at the seven wooden blocks. He had read many books about the **Maori** people during his studies, so he surely knew the answer. He just had to be able to recall it. Prince **Gem of Ology** grabbed the letters and slowly rearranged them, one block at a time. Playing with the order of the letters, he moved and shuffled them back and forth.

Manoupu? he thought. *No. Umanoup? No.*

Suddenly, he remembered. Stepping aside, he proudly presented his reply - P, O, U, N, A, M and U.

"**Pounamu**!" the steward exclaimed excitedly. "Excellent, Your Majesty! You did it! You solved the very last puzzle!" With that, the steward handed Prince **Gem of Ology** a tiny wooden box. Carefully opening its lid, the Prince's eyes fell upon a rich green gem. Never before had he seen such a magnificent piece of **Jade**.

"Go on," the steward said. "Place the gem with all your others." Opening his velvet pouch, Prince **Gem of Ology** gently placed the last of the ten gems inside it. As soon as he let the gem fall into his pouch, an enormously bright bolt of blazing light crackled overhead and pierced its way through the twilight sky. Blinded by its intense glare, the Prince threw his arms over his head.

Then, everything around him was absolutely still.

Slowly lowering his arms, Prince **Gem of Ology** couldn't believe his eyes. He no longer stood amongst the sweet smelling flowers of the meadow. Instead, he found himself in his father's magnificent palace, amidst hundreds of applauding subjects. The halls trembled with cheering and shouts of excitement.

An old and wise-looking man stepped forward. With a golden scepter in his hands and an ornate crown upon his head, he said, "Welcome back, my dear son. Today is the most glorious day of all, for 'tis my day to resign and to proudly present this land with its new and worthy King. With your victorious quest you have proven to understand and know about this kingdom's diverse regions and its native people, the most essential attribute of a wise and prosperous King."

The King clapped his hands, and he was brought a pillow. Upon it sat the most breathtaking and magnificent crown anybody within the kingdom of **Paragon** had ever seen. Ten beautiful jewels adorned the crown, each placed on its own prong.

"These, my son, are the jewels you acquired during your

quest today. Each one represents a different people within our lands. You indeed have proven yourself worthy to leading the kingdom of **Paragon**."

With these words, the King lifted the crown from the pillow and placed it on his son's head. "May the kingdom of **Paragon** prosper and thrive under your royal guidance, King **Gem of the House of Ology**. Hip, hip, hooray! Hip, hip, hooray!"

A wave of deafening applause and cheerfulness arose once more, like a parade of a thousand elephants. They feasted and they drank, and were merry and of good spirits. And King **Gem of Ology** lived long and happily, and ruled his people well.

The End

GLOSSARY

Adamas: From ancient Greek, meaning *diamond-like, unbreakable, unalterable*

Amethyst: Violet variety of quartz; most valued quartz variety; Greek for *not drunken*

Bacchus: Because of its wine-like color, early Greek legends associated Amethysts with Bacchus, the god of wine

Beryl: A mineral species; occurs in a diversity of colors; has several important gemstone varieties such as Emerald and Aquamarine

Capao: One of the oldest and most productive fully mechanized Imperial topaz mines in the historic Ouro Preto area of Minas Gerais in Brazil

Ceylon: Now called *Sri Lanka*; island southeast of India; The Ceylon blue sapphires are famous for their brightness and vibrant colors

Coober Pedy: "Opal capital of the world," Australia; comes from the local Aboriginal term *kupa-piti*, which means "boys' waterhole"

Corundum: Aluminum oxide; Ruby and Sapphire are varieties of corundum

Diamond: The only gem made of a single element (Carbon); the hardest substance on earth; from ancient Greek, meaning *unbreakable*

Emerald: Term derived from an ancient Persian word that translated to the Greek as *Smaragdus*, meaning *green stone*; bluish green to green variety of Beryl (see above)

Gemology: Science that studies gems

Imperial Topaz: Lustrous golden orange-yellow, orange-brown, or orange-pink variety of Topaz; the most valuable kind

Jade: Latin for *flanks, kidney area*; used from prehistoric periods for hardstone carving

Krustallos: word *crystal* is derived from the Ancient Greek word κρύσταλλος (krustallos), meaning both "ice" and "rock crystal"

Maori:	The indigenous Polynesian people of New Zealand; considered Jade a treasure and therefore protected it under the Treaty of Waitangi
Mefkat:	Ancient Egyptians called Turquoise "mefkat," which also means "joy" and "delight"
Mogok:	The valley of Mogok, Burma, has been yielding the world's most beautiful Rubies and Sapphires
Momme:	A unit for measuring the weight of Pearls
Mystic Topaz:	Multicolored Topaz with a rainbow-like color effect
Opal:	A gemstone consisting of hydrated silica; typically semitransparent, showing varying colors against a pale or dark ground
Paragon:	A perfect Diamond of 100 carats or more; a person or thing viewed as a model of excellence
Pearl:	A hard object produced within the soft tissue of a living shelled mollusk
Persian Blue:	Term for turquoise of this beautiful color
Pounamu:	The Maori (see above) name for Jade
Ruby:	From the Latin word "ruber," which means *red*; the most valuable variety of the corundum mineral species
Sapphire:	Typically blue gemstone variety of the mineral corundum
Sherry Topaz:	Topaz with a light orange-brown to brownish-pink color
Smaragdus:	From ancient Greek, meaning *green precious stone*;
Topaz:	A silicate mineral of aluminum and fluorine; pure topaz is colorless and transparent but is usually tinted by impurities
Turquoise:	From the French expression *Pierre Tourques*, or *Turkish Stone*; typically opaque and of a greenish-blue or sky-blue color, consisting of a hydrated hydroxyl phosphate of copper and aluminum

ABOUT THE AUTHOR

Yvonne Jones was born in former East Germany to a German mother and a Vietnamese father. Thus, she spent an inordinate amount of her youth nosing through books that she shouldn't have been reading, and watching movies that she shouldn't have been watching. It was a good childhood.

Always drawing inspiration from her own two children, she loves to write about unique interests and aspires to find fun and exciting ways to have kids discover and learn about the magnificent marvels this world has to offer.

She can be found online at www.Yvonne-Jones.com.

A WORD BY THE AUTHOR

If you enjoyed this book, it would be wonderful if you could take a short minute to leave a lovely review on Amazon, as your kind feedback is very appreciated and so very important. It gives me, the author, encouragement for bad days when I want to take up scorpion petting. Thank you so very much for your time!

MORE WORKS BY THIS AUTHOR

The Case of the Mona Lisa – The Amulet of Amser Series (1)
The Case of the Starry Night – The Amulet of Amser Series (2)
The Case of Venus de Milo – The Amulet of Amser Series (3)
The Impatient Little Vacuum
Safety Goose: Children's Safety – One Rhyme at a Time ***
Growing Up in East Germany – My Childhood Series (1)
Teeny Totty Uses Mama's Big Potty: Transition from Potty Chair to Toilet
Got Garbage? The Garbage Book for the Biggest Garbage Fan

*** Visit **www.Yvonne-Jones.com** to receive a FREE eBook version of this book

www.ingramcontent.com/pod-product-compliance
Lightning Source LLC
Chambersburg PA
CBHW061931290426
44113CB00024B/2874